WHAT I BELIEVE

Alan Brown and Andrew Langley

The Millbrook Press   Brookfield, Connecticut

THE MILLBROOK PRESS

© Copyright 1999 Transedition Limited & Fernleigh Books
All rights reserved including the right of reproduction in whole or in part in any form.

First published in the United States of America in 1999 by Millbrook Press Inc., 2 Old New Milford Road, Brookfield CT 06804

Library of Congress Cataloging-in-Publication Data

Brown, Alan, 1944-
    What I believe: a young person's guide to the religions of the world/ Alan Brown and Andrew Langley.
        p.   cm.
    Includes index.
    Summary: Introduces Judaism, Christianity, Islam, Hinduism, Buddhism, Sikhism, Shinto, and Taoism through the eyes of young members of those faiths.

    10 9 8 7 6 5 4 3 2
    ISBN 0-7613-1501-2   Hardcover

    10 9 8 7 6 5 4 3 2 1
    ISBN 0-7613-1448-2   Paperback

    1. Religions--Juvenile literature. [1. Religions.] I. Langley, Andrew. II. Title.
BL92.B755 1999
291--dc21   98-33120
                                                  CIP
    Printed in Italy   AC

Credits

What I Believe was produced for Transedition Limited & Fernleigh Books by Lionheart Books.

Project Manager: Lionel Bender
Designer and Art Editor: Ben White
Text Editors: Alison Freegard and Michael March
Make-up: Mike Pilley, Pelican Graphics
Picture Research: Jennie Karrach and
    Lionel Bender

Main Artwork: Teri Gower
Historical Artwork: Mark Bergin
Studio Photography: Steve Gorton, with John
    Moulder and Louise Taylor
Religious symbols and items provided by
    Artefacts to Order, England.

Publishing Director: Edward Glover
Production: Richard Johnson
Cover Design: Mike Pilley, Pelican Graphics

Consultants:
Martin E. Marty – Professor Emeritus, The
    University of Chicago and Director of the Public
    Religion Project.
The National Society (Church of England)
    for Promoting Religious Education, London,
    England – special thanks to Alison Seaman
    and Alan Brown.

Contents

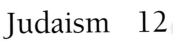

Religion Today

There are many different religions in the world. Most people follow one of these religions. They keep its festivals and teach their children the basic beliefs. We will follow a group of children as they introduce us to their religions. They will tell and show us the basic stories, customs, beliefs, and traditions of their faith. Yet, within each religion, some people will do one thing while others do something else. For many people religion is part of everyday life. It is not a special service at a special time of the year.

Hinduism

I am a Hindu girl. My family comes from India. I am wearing the clothes I wear every day. We believe God is in everything, but my family especially worships the God Krishna. My faith is part of my everyday life.

Judaism

I am a Jewish boy. My family comes from Israel. Israel is a special country for Jews. We believe God chose us to be his special people and live in Israel. I wear a *yarmulke* or *kippah*, a skull cap, on my head. It is an important Jewish symbol.

Taoism

I am a Chinese boy. I follow the Taoist way of life. We pronounce our religion as "Dow." We have great respect for our elders. They are believed to be very wise and teach us a good way of life.

Islam

I am a Muslim girl. My family comes from the Middle East. I wear a *hijab* over my head like my mother. My religion is Islam. We believe there is only one God and Muhammad is God's messenger.

Sikhism

I am a Sikh boy. When I am older, I will join the *khalsa*, which is the Sikh community. I will then wear the *turban*. I do not cut my hair. I live in England, but my family comes from the Punjab in India.

Shintoism

I am a Japanese girl. I and my family follow the Shinto way of life. We believe in having great respect for our elders. I live with my brother, parents, grandparents, and an aunt. Most people who are Shinto live in Japan.

Christianity

I am a Christian girl. I live in the United States. I go to church and believe in the teaching of Jesus Christ. I wear a cross around my neck to show I am a Christian.

Buddhism

I am a Buddhist. My family and I now live in Thailand. It is a custom here that when I am a bit older I will have my head shaved. I will go into a monastery for a short time. We follow the teaching of the Buddha.

As we can see, the children have both similar and different beliefs. Some of the children wear special clothes or special symbols on chains round their necks. We can see immediately which religion they belong to. Religions such as Christianity and Islam emphasize the importance of a particular historical person. Other religions, for example Taoism, do not have a special person and instead follow teachings and customs handed down over many years. We are going to follow our children as they lead us through some of the most important events in their lives.

What is a Religion?

People often say they are religious but find it hard to explain what that means. Most religions have a belief in a god. They believe that, somehow, the god made everything. These people say prayers, worship, and try to learn more about their faith. Other religions do not believe in a god. They believe they should follow a way of life in which they treat everyone with respect.

Comparing clothes and religious symbols

Food

Every religion has special foods for special occasions, such as certain fruits at harvest time. Many Hindus are vegetarian: they do not eat meat. Jews and Muslims will eat some foods but not others, and only if they are prepared in a special way. Jews and Muslims will not eat pork, for example.

Buddhist boys and priest in a monastery

At school meals, Muslim, Hindu, Sikh, and Christian children will choose different foods.

Clothes

Sometimes, religious people wear special clothes. A Sikh man will wear shorts under his trousers. A Jewish man will wear a *yarmulke* and sometimes a prayer shawl in the synagogue. A Christian priest will wear special clothing for religious services in church. Muslims in the Middle and Far East wear long, loose robes. At times we can tell what religion people are from their clothes—but not always.

Hindu children pray before the shrine in their living room

Around the Home

When we walk into a house we can often tell what religion a person is. A Jewish home will have a *mezuzah* on the doorpost. A Christian home may have a cross, *crucifix*, or picture of Jesus. In the Hindu home there will be a statue of a god. People live their faith at home.

Symbols

Most people have in their homes photographs of people they love and think about. So religious people will have symbols of their religion. There may be a *menorah* (a special candle holder) in a Jewish home, or a picture of a saint or a cross in a Christian home. Muslims have a holy book that is handled with great care.

Making greeting cards and symbols for each other's festivals

To prepare for his Sabbath, our Jewish child goes home early on a Friday afternoon.

Festivals

Everyone likes to celebrate. Hindus seem to have festivals every day, but India is a big country and someone somewhere has a special event to be happy about. Whether celebrating the birth of the Buddha, Easter, Passover, or Id-ul-Fitr, a good time is had by all in each religion. Usually festivals celebrate a time of importance in the religion's history.

7

Early Beliefs and Traditions

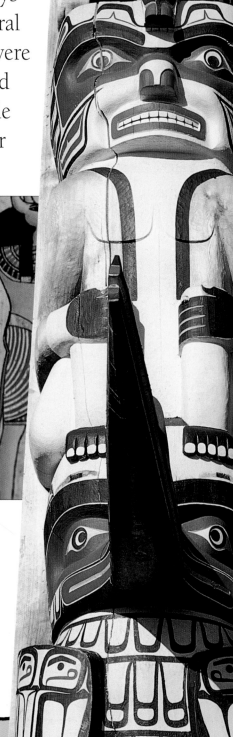

A totem pole in western Canada showing people and animals

No one is sure how religions began, but they have always been a part of every tribe and region of the world. Several countries have temples, shrines, and prayer halls that were built more than 2,000 years ago. There, people gathered to worship and share their mystical beliefs. Some people say cave paintings and standing stones dating from over 5,000 years ago were part of religious customs. Others say these are art and not really religious symbols.

Wood Carvings

Native Americans are famous for totem poles. When European explorers first met Native Americans, they thought these people had no religion. They did not realize that the totem poles were put up to remember events, to honor dead relatives, or to keep away evil spirits. Today, many people in the world use Native American prayers and sayings.

We can learn about our religions by looking at ancient beliefs.

Cave Paintings

One of the most exciting recent discoveries is a cave with ancient paintings on the walls. The paintings were done thousands of years ago. Are they religious? Some people say yes, because it shows our ancestors wanted power over animals to catch and eat them. Other people say we can't be certain that the paintings have anything to do with religious beliefs.

Cave painting of a horse and hands

An ancient Egyptian wall painting of gods and goddesses

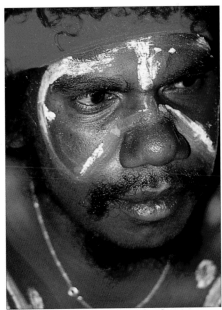

Aborigines paint themselves with plant pigments as part of Dreamtime, in which they remember their ancestors. They believe their ancestors never died but became part of nature and live on in their sacred traditions.

Beliefs and Ideas

When we think of religions, we often think of religions such as Islam, Christianity, and Judaism. These have firm traditions, customs, prayers, and holidays. The Aborigine people of Australia have a different sort of religion. They have developed skills to live in the desert. They live very close to nature. They still cling to their old practices and a belief in Dreamtime. Their religion is a way of thinking about being part of the world around them.

Holy Writings

Some religions have a book or books that tell us about their faith. These usually contain stories and teachings. They are a guide to how believers should live. People read from these books or act out the stories.

Buddhism

Buddhists have many scriptures. The most important are the *Tripitaka*. They contain the teachings of the Buddha and his followers. Among these are the Four Noble Truths and the Eightfold Path.

Buddhist boy

Judaism

The holy book of Jews is known as the *Bible*. It is written in Hebrew, and is divided into three sections. The most important section is called the *Torah*. It is written on scrolls, not paper. It contains the teachings that God gave to the prophet Moses. Among them are the Ten Commandments.

Jewish boy holding *Torah* scrolls

The *Torah* scrolls

Sikhism

The most important scripture is the *Guru Granth Sahib*. It contains hymns about Sikh beliefs and traditions. It is written in Gurmukhi, a language similar to Punjabi. Sikhs treat the *Guru Granth Sahib* with great respect.

Sikh boy with *Guru Granth Sahib*

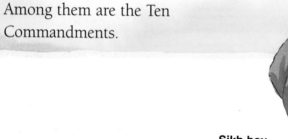

Shintoism

Unlike some of the other religions, the beliefs and customs of Shinto are not in a book. The traditions are passed on through the family.

Taoism

This way of life relies on many books. But one has become famous, the *Tao Te Ching*. It is a book of poetry and ideas about learning. It is written in Chinese.

Christianity

The Christian holy book is called the *Bible*. It has two parts, the *Old Testament* and the *New Testament*. The *Old Testament* is almost the same as the Jewish *Bible*. The *New Testament* tells of the importance of the life and death of Jesus for Christians.

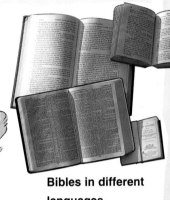

Bibles in different languages

Shinto girl

Taoist boy

Christian girl holding a *Bible*

Hinduism

The religious books of the Hindus contain stories, prayers, hymns, and poems. They are written in Sanskrit, the language of ancient India. Hindus have a favorite story or prayer. The acting out of the stories is how children learn them.

Islam

The Muslim book is called the *Qur'an* (also written as *Koran*). Muslims believe it contains the words of Allah, or God, as given to the prophet Muhammad. The *Qur'an* is written in Arabic.

Hindu girl

Muslim girl

11

The Story of Judaism

Our Jewish faith began more than 4,000 years ago in the Middle East. At that time, people worshiped many different gods. But a man named Abraham believed that there was only one God. He spoke to God and made a covenant, or bargain, with God. Abraham and his family promised to worship and obey God. In return, God promised to make them The Chosen People. God guided Abraham's descendants to a new land called Canaan, where they grew into a great nation—the Jewish people.

Moses comes back down from Mount Sinai. He carries two stone tablets that God has given him. The Ten Laws, or Commandments, are written on the tablets.

The Torah

The story of how the Jewish faith began is told in the *Torah*. The *Torah* includes the first five books of the Hebrew *Bible*. We read part of it at every service. The *Torah* tells how a Jew named Moses led his people from slavery in Egypt back to their promised land. On the way, God called Moses to the top of a mountain. There, God gave Moses a set of laws for the Jewish people to live by. These laws are also part of the *Torah* we read today.

The Ten Commandments

1. Worship no god but Me.
2. Do not make idols to worship.
3. Do not use the name of God for evil things.
4. Keep the Sabbath day holy.
5. Respect your father and mother.
6. Do not murder.
7. Do not go with another man's wife.
8. Do not steal.
9. Do not accuse anyone falsely.
10. Do not envy what other people have.

The Western Wall

Jews worship and pray at the Western Wall in Jerusalem. This was once part of a great temple. Jerusalem had become the capital city of Israel, with many beautiful buildings. Then, about 2,000 years ago, the Romans conquered the land. The Jews rebelled against the invaders, but were defeated. The Romans destroyed the Temple, and only the Western Wall was left standing.

Jews pray at the Western Wall

Hebrew

There is a copy of the *Torah* in every Jewish synagogue (meeting place). The words are written by hand, from right to left, in a language called Hebrew. We begin reading the *Torah* at the festival of Simchat Torah, and read a section each Sabbath. By the end of the year, we will have read the whole *Torah*.

Touching the Mezuzah

Every time I go through a doorway in my house, I reach up and touch the *mezuzah*. This is a small box fixed to the doorpost. Inside it is a tiny scroll with the words of a special prayer and passages from the *Torah*. Some grown-ups kiss the *mezuzah*, but I'm not tall enough! So, after I have touched the *mezuzah*, I kiss my fingers instead. Fixing these words to your doorposts is to honor and remember God.

Being Jewish

The two most important places for a Jew are the home and the synagogue. At home, we learn about our religion in all sorts of everyday things. We also celebrate many festivals at home, especially the Sabbath, and talk about what we have read in the scriptures. Our synagogue is the place where we can meet together and worship God. I also go there with other children to learn Hebrew and study the *Torah*.

The Rabbi

Rabbis are teachers who are trained to know all about Jewish law. They help us study the Torah. They also give advice and comfort, and answer questions about our faith. In some synagogues, men only can become rabbis; in others, women can be rabbis too.

In the Synagogue

We go to a service in the synagogue every Friday evening and Saturday morning. Men cover their heads as a sign of respect to God. The cantor stands up on the *bimah* (platform) to lead the service. Behind him or her is a special cupboard called the Ark. This is where the Torah is kept. The Torah is written by hand on scrolls, which often have a velvet cover decorated with silver. A lamp, called the eternal light, always burns over the Ark.

My Family Sabbath

The seventh day of the Jewish week is called the Sabbath, our day of rest. It begins at dusk on Friday, when my family has a special meal. We light two Sabbath candles, drink a little wine, and eat some bread. We like to be together on the Sabbath. The Sabbath ends on Saturday evening, when we light a single candle.

Signs of Faith

In the synagogue, many Jewish men wear special symbols to show their faith. The *yarmulke*, or skull cap, covers the head. The *tallit* is a fringed prayer shawl. Orthodox men wear *tefillin*, which are tiny boxes with scrolls written with words from the *Torah*, strapped to the forehead and arm. They also wear *tsitsit*, which are tassels on a vest worn under the shirt. The Star of David is worn on a chain round the neck.

Jewish Food

There are strict rules about what we eat and how we prepare our food. Meat must be killed and treated by a special butcher to make it *kosher* (proper). Jews must not eat milk foods after meat at the same meal. In our kitchen there are two refrigerators: one is for meat foods, the other for dairy foods.

Tefillin **bag**

Tefillin

Tallit

Yarmulke

Star of David

Tsitsit

The Year

We have our own calendar. Jewish months last from one new moon to the next. This makes them shorter than ordinary months, so in some years we add an extra month to catch up. There are many Jewish festivals during the year. These help us to remember important times in our history, with stories, songs, or special foods.

On the *seder* plate are an egg, parsley, horse radish, a roasted lamb bone, saltwater, and a mix of apple, nut, and cinnamon. Each is a symbol of the Passover story.

Purim: February/March

Esther was a Jewish queen long ago in Persia (Iran). She saved her people from an evil man called Haman. On Purim we dress up as kings and queens and listen as Esther's story is read in the synagogue. Whenever Haman's name is mentioned, we all boo and stamp our feet!

Passover: March/April

Pesach, or Passover, celebrates the time when the Israelites escaped from slavery in Egypt. This festival lasts eight days, beginning with a special meal called a *seder*. We also eat a flat bread called *matzoh*, just as our ancestors did on their journey.

Sukkot: October

This is our harvest festival, when we remember the homes our ancestors made in the desert during their flight to the Promised Land. We build *sukkot* (shelters) in our gardens and decorate them with fruit and branches. We spend most of the seven days in our *sukkah*.

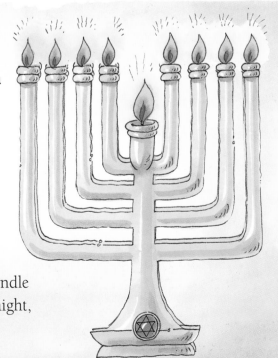

Yom Kippur: September/October

This is our day of repentance. We pray in the synagogue to say we are sorry to God and to each other for what we have done wrong. At home, we light a candle that burns for 25 hours. During that time, grown-ups "fast" (go without food and drink). The *shofar* is blown at the end of the fast.

Rosh Hoshanah: September

This is our New Year. Each morning, someone in the synagogue blows the *shofar* (ram's horn) to remind us of the things we did wrong last year. At home we eat apple dipped in honey to wish each other a sweet new year.

Hanukkah: December

Over 2,000 years ago, the Israelites defeated a wicked king who had made them give up their religion. To celebrate the victory, the Temple was opened again. But there was only enough oil for the Temple lamp to burn for one day. All the same, the lamp was lit—and, amazingly, kept burning for eight whole days. At Hanukkah, we light candles in a special candlestick called a *menorah*. There are eight main branches—one for each day of the festival—and a branch to hold a candle used to light the others. One candle is lit on the first night, two on the second, and so on.

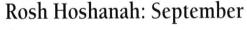

Growing Up

There are two ways to become a Jew. One is to be born into a Jewish family. The other way is to convert—to choose and learn to follow the Jewish faith. You can do this at any age. When you follow the Jewish way of life, each important stage of your life is marked with a special event. The first is when you are born and welcomed by family and friends in the synagogue. Your parents give you a Jewish name. As soon as you can speak, your mother teaches you the words of our daily prayer, the *shema*. Then, when you are five years old, you go to classes at the synagogue to learn about the Jewish faith. You learn to read and write Hebrew, too.

Circumcision

Eight days after he is born, a Jewish boy is circumcised to remember Abraham's covenant with God and Isaac's story. A specially trained person called a *mohel* cuts the foreskin from the boy's penis. As he does this, the *mohel* recites a blessing. The baby boy is given a little wine to calm him. After the circumcision, the boy is given his Hebrew name, and the family has a celebration.

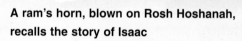

A ram's horn, blown on Rosh Hoshanah, recalls the story of Isaac

Abraham and Isaac

God wanted to make sure that Abraham would always stay faithful. So God gave him a test. God ordered Abraham to kill Isaac, his son, and burn him on an altar as a sacrifice to God. Abraham obeyed God and was ready to kill his young son. This proved to God that Abraham would do anything God asked. At the last moment, God told Abraham to stop and to let Isaac go. Looking round, Abraham saw a ram with its horns caught in a bush, and killed that in place of his son. As a reward, God promised to bless Abraham and his family.

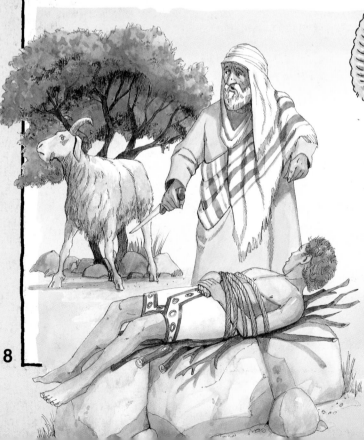

Bar and Bat Mitzvah

When I am 13 years old, I will become a grown-up. This means that I must behave properly and follow the laws of the Jewish faith. A boy of this age is called *bar mitzvah* (son of the commandment). Jewish girls grow up quicker! At 12 years of age, a girl becomes *bat mitzvah* (daughter of the commandment). In a special service at the synagogue, the boy or girl chants the blessings before and after the *Torah* is read.

Marriage

Before a wedding, the bride and groom sign a *ketubah* (wedding contract). This promises that they will always care for each other. At a ceremony under a canopy, the groom puts a gold ring on the bride's finger. The rabbi blesses the couple, and the groom breaks a wine glass under his foot. This reminds us of how the Temple was destroyed long ago. After the wedding, there is usually a meal and dancing.

Death

When a Jew dies, he or she is buried quickly. The body is washed and wrapped in a white sheet, put in a coffin, then placed in a Jewish cemetery. Afterward, the family of the dead person stay at home for a week to mourn. Old Hebrew books and a *Torah* may be buried with the person.

Jews Around the World

A modern synagogue in the United States

There are about 14 million Jews in the world. About half live in the U.S.A. There are only 4 million Jews in Israel. There are nearly 2.5 million Jews in Russia and the former Soviet republics. There are many Jews in Europe, especially in France (about 530,000) and Britain (about 300,000). Judaism is a worldwide religion, with small numbers of Jews in India, Canada, Brazil, Argentina, and South Africa.

Branches of Judaism

Sephardic Jews have ancestors who lived mostly in Spain about 600 years ago. Ashkenazi Jews have ancestors who lived in what are now Russia and Poland about 200 years ago. In each of these groups, there are three main types—Orthodox, Conservative, and Reform.

Orthodox Jews

Orthodox Jews are traditionalists. We often call the very orthodox Lubavich, after the town of the same name they originally came from. They are part of Hassidic Judaism, which began in eastern Europe. Hassids hold to traditional beliefs, customs, and religious practices that have been handed down for centuries. They are very studious and learned, and tend to believe in the historical truth of the Hebrew *Bible*. Most Hassidic Jews live in Eastern Europe, North America, and Israel.

Conservative Jews

Conservative Jews also believe in traditional Jewish values, but they are more open to the modern way of everyday life. They will probably use less Hebrew during synagogue worship and wear clothes that do not distinguish them from Gentiles (non-Jews). There are large numbers of Conservative Jews in North America and Europe.

A rabbi helps girls study the *Torah* in a Lubavich school

Reform Jews

The Reform Jews take the *Bible* very seriously, but most of them do not consider it to be literally true. They use little Hebrew in their synagogue services, and observe only some of the festivals. Most Reform Jews live in Europe and North America.

The Diaspora

Diaspora is a term meaning the scattering of the Jews. Jews are spread over the world, mainly because they have always had to flee from anti-Semitism. More than 2,500 years ago, Jews were persecuted and taken from Israel to Babylon (now part of Iraq).

Occasionally, the world hears of a Jewish group that time has passed by. The Falashas of Ethiopia were one such group. They seemed to keep many Jewish practices, but lived isolated from other Jews. This small group, who were not Sephardic or Ashkenazi, were living proof of the diversity of Judaism in all its traditions. Most Falashas now live in Israel.

A family of Falashas

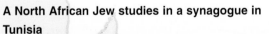

A North African Jew studies in a synagogue in Tunisia

The Holocaust

In this century, during the Second World War, about six million Jews were killed by the Nazis. This is called the Holocaust (or *Shoah*). Jewish people of Germany and other European countries invaded by Germany were put into concentration camps, and many were killed because of their faith and their race. It was this terrible period that encouraged the Jews of the world to work together to found the modern state of Israel in 1948.

The State of Israel

Jews believe they are God's chosen people and that God gave them the land of Israel. Israel is very special to Jews because most of Jewish history took place in this "Holy Land." In Jerusalem, the Western Wall of Herod's Temple is a place of pilgrimage for Jews from all over the world. Not all Israelis are Jews, but the very orthodox Jews have a powerful influence on the way the country is run. Whatever differences there are among Jews, they all believe passionately in the State of Israel and talk of meeting "Next year in Jerusalem."

The Story of Christianity

We are called Christians because we follow the teaching of Jesus Christ. Jesus was a Jew, born about 2,000 years ago in the part of the Middle East now called Israel. We believe that Jesus was the Son of God, who came to live on earth. He told people that God had created the world to show God's power and love for them. We believe that Jesus lives on today.

The Sermon on the Mount

For three years, Jesus traveled about, teaching people to love God and obey God's laws. A band of twelve close followers, called disciples, went with him. Huge crowds gathered to listen to Jesus. One day, there were so many people that he climbed onto a hill, or mount, to speak to them. Jesus said that God blessed anyone who was meek, gentle, and merciful. "Love your enemies," he said, "and do good to those who hate you."

Death and New Life

Many people loved Jesus, but others mistrusted him. The Roman rulers thought he was plotting a rebellion. Religious leaders thought he was breaking Jewish laws. The Romans arrested him and put him on trial. Jesus was sentenced to death by being crucified (nailed to a wooden cross). His dead body was placed in a cave, with a big stone blocking the entrance. Three days later, some women saw that the stone had been rolled away, and that Jesus' body was gone. An angel appeared and told them that Jesus was alive. Soon, more of his followers saw him. They believed that he was raised from the dead by the power of God. This is called Jesus' Resurrection.

The Trinity

Christians believe in one God, like the Jews. But we say that God comes to us as three "persons"—God the Father, God the Son (Jesus), and God the Holy Spirit. These are called the Holy Trinity (three parts). This painting shows God the Father as a cloud high in the heavens, and the Holy Spirit as a dove. God the Son is a baby, being held in the arms of Mary, his mother. Some Christians, such as Roman Catholics, are deeply devoted to Mary because she was the Mother of God.

Some people devote their lives to God by joining communities of monks (men) or nuns (women). These nuns and children are at a school in Zimbabwe, Africa.

The Cross

A cross is the symbol of the Christian faith, reminding us that Jesus died for our sake. Many of us like to wear a cross on a neck chain. This painted cross to hang on a wall comes from a Greek Orthodox church. A cross may show a fish, which is also a symbol of Christianity: one story tells how Jesus fed 5,000 people with just two fish and five loaves of bread.

The Bible

The first part of the *Bible* is the *Old Testament*. Its books are the writings of the Hebrew prophets. It is shared by Christians and Jews. The *New Testament* contains Jesus' teachings, given in the *Gospels*. These are the writings of Matthew, Mark, Luke, and John. They are sometimes called the *Evangelists*, which means "announcers of good news."

Being a Christian

The local church is at the heart of every Christian community. We go there to worship God with our fellow Christians every Sunday, and sometimes on other days as well. Many Christians prefer to keep Sunday a day of rest, when no work should be done.

Praying

We say our prayers every night before we go to bed. Praying is a way of talking to God, describing our lives and problems, and asking God for guidance and help. In church, we say special prayers from a book. All Christians know the Lord's Prayer, which begins, "Our Father who art (is) in Heaven."

Inside a Church

The church service is led by the priest or by a pastor. Our church is big so the priest has an assistant to help him. The priest stands in front of the altar (a table) on which there are candles and a small cross. I sit in the choir and like to look at the east window —it faces toward Jerusalem, Christianity's most holy city. Some churches are just a simple room, or even a hut.

The Last Supper

Our most important ceremony has many names: Holy Communion, Mass, the Last Supper, and the Lord's Supper. This celebrates the death and resurrection of Jesus. The *Bible* story tells us that Jesus knew he was soon going to be arrested and put to death. He ate a final meal with his twelve disciples. This is often called the Last Supper. During the meal, Jesus told his disciples that one of them would betray him (this was Judas). Giving each one a piece of bread, Jesus said, "This is my body." Then Jesus gave them wine, saying, "This is my blood."

"The Last Supper"—as shown in a painting by a Dutch artist who lived more than 450 years ago

Communion

When remembering Jesus' Last Supper by sharing bread and wine at a service of Holy Communion, we believe that Jesus is with us in a special way. The priest or pastor blesses the bread and wine, and gives each person a piece of bread (this is often a wafer) and a sip of wine from a special Communion cup. Often the priest asks children who are too young to take part to come to the altar to be blessed.

Communion wine

Communion cup

Bread—with a portion torn off to give to eat

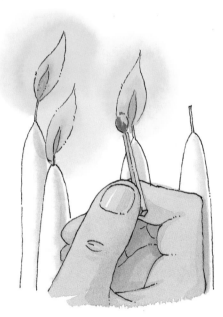

Remembering

Many Christians, including Anglicans, Orthodox, and Roman Catholics, light a candle when they enter a church. The light of the candle shows that they have remembered a loved one who has died, or the anniversary of a saint (a very holy person). There are special candles to celebrate festivals such as Christmas and Easter.

The Christian Year

Many of our festivals recall events from the life of Jesus, from his birth at Christmas to his death and new life at Easter. Forty days after Easter comes Ascension Day, when we believe Jesus was lifted up to Heaven.

Advent and Christmas (December)

During Advent we get ready to celebrate Jesus' birthday. We practice singing Christmas hymns called carols. Advent begins about a month before Christmas. Some Christians burn special candles on each Sunday during Advent. On Christmas Day itself, we go to a church service. Afterward, we give each other presents and eat a special Christmas meal. Twelve days after Christmas, we celebrate Epiphany, to remember the arrival at Bethlehem of the three wise men.

The Nativity

The *Gospels* of Luke and Matthew tell the traditional story of the birth of Jesus. Near the time of the birth, Mary and Joseph were on their way to Bethlehem. The town was so crowded that they had to sleep in a stable. That night, Mary gave birth to Jesus. There was no bed, so she put the baby in a manger (where the animals eat their hay). Shepherds came from nearby to worship the child they believed to be the Son of God. And three wise men traveled to Bethlehem from far in the East, guided by a bright new star.

At Christmas, we send greetings cards to our relatives and friends. We also make a model crib, like the one in the stable where Jesus was born. We decorate our homes with holly, candles, and a Christmas fir tree.

Lent (February/March)

There are several festivals that lead up to our celebration of the death and resurrection of Jesus at Easter. First comes Lent, when we remember the forty days Jesus spent alone and hungry in the desert. We pray and fast. In some countries, the day before Lent is a festival called Mardi Gras, or Shrove Tuesday. People stage carnivals, where they dress in brilliant costumes, and parade or dance through the streets.

Mardi Gras celebrations in Bolivia, South America

Easter lilies – to remind us that Jesus is the Prince of Peace

Palm cross

Easter eggs

Holy Week (March/April)

When Jesus entered Jerusalem, people covered his path with palm leaves and palm branches. On Palm Sunday, at the start of Holy Week, we are given palm-leaf crosses to remind us of this. Easter candles are burned through the week. On Good Friday, we remember Jesus' Crucifixion, and on Easter Sunday, we celebrate his return to life. Many people give each other chocolate or painted Easter eggs, which are symbols of new life.

Christian girls in Sweden celebrate Saint Lucia's Day

Saints' Days

For many Christians, a saint is any true believer in Christ. To others, saints are men and women who have lived holy lives, performed miracles, or been of great service to their faith and religious community. There are hundreds of saints, and festivals are held for many of them in different parts of the world. There is at least one saints' day on each day of the year.

Some saints are linked with countries, some with activities. So St. Patrick is the patron saint of Ireland.

Many Christians think of St. Christopher, who helped the young Jesus cross a stream, as the patron saint of travelers. Some Christians celebrate Halloween (All Hallows Eve), the night before All Saints' Day, November 1. The next day, November 2, is All Souls' Day, when some Christians honor and pray for relatives and friends who have died.

Growing Up

At birth, most churches baptize to bring us into the faith, but some "dedicate" us, or turn us over, to God until we are old enough to decide to be baptized. Later, we confirm our vows, or promises. Christian couples make their marriage promises in church. A funeral service is held here when someone dies.

Being Baptized

We all stand around the *font* (a special basin). The priest places a few drops of holy water (water that has been blessed) onto my baby brother's forehead, then traces the sign of the cross. In other churches, baptism takes place when you are an adult and old enough to make the promises yourself.

Some adults are baptized by being immersed in water in a church or in a lake or river.

A Christening

Babies are usually baptized when they are a few weeks old. Of course, they are still too young to know about the Christian faith, but baptism is a sign that they belong to God. At the Christening, the baby is given his or her first, or Christian, names. The parents choose other adults to be the baby's godparents. They make promises to be good Christians on behalf of the baby.

Many Christians are given a *Bible* or a *Prayer Book* when they are baptized. Some will receive *rosary* beads—the large beads remind them of the Lord's Prayer and the small beads the prayers to Mary, the Mother of Jesus.

Confirmation

After we turn seven years old, we can confirm the promises that were made for us at our baptism. We go to classes where we are taught about the Christian faith and the Holy Communion service. At the confirmation ceremony, a priest lays his hands on our head and welcomes us into God's family. After this, we can receive communion bread and wine for the first time.

Girls in Malta dressed for Confirmation

At Holy Communion, the priest or pastor gives us each a wafer.

Marriage

Being married in church is a happy occasion. My aunt is wearing a beautiful dress with a long train, which we bridesmaids are carrying. The bride and bridegroom say to the priest, and to their families and friends, that they promise to love and care for each other all their lives. Then they give each other a ring. After the ceremony, there is a big feast. The guests give presents to the newly married couple.

Death and Burial

For a Christian, death is not the end of life, because Jesus promised that anyone who believes in him will be given everlasting life. When a person dies, the body is placed in a coffin. After a funeral service, the coffin may be buried, with a cross or stone to mark the place, or the body may be cremated.

Christians Around the World

There are more than 1.7 billion Christians spread all over the world. Christianity is the world's largest religion. Christians belong to 22,000 different groups or churches! The biggest group is the Roman Catholic Church: there are about 900 million Catholics. The rest are mainly Protestant or Orthodox.

The Pope on a visit to Britain

The Orthodox Church

Orthodox Christians believe that whatever happens in the world, worship of God must continue because that is what is expected. There are fifteen Orthodox Churches, mostly in Eastern Europe and Russia, but also in North America. All are equal and independent. They are usually named after countries, for example, Russian Orthodox and Greek Orthodox. However, the *patriarch* (religious leader) in Istanbul, Turkey, is given the greatest honor.

A Greek Orthodox Communion service

Roman Catholics

The word catholic means universal, but there are several types of Catholicism. Roman Catholics agree that the *pope* in the Vatican in Rome is head of the Church. He has this title because he links his authority back to Peter, Jesus' chief disciple, and so to Jesus himself. There are Roman Catholics in every country in the world and they all look to Rome for guidance.

Protestant children singing hymns in church

Pilgrimages

Many Christians celebrate their shared beliefs by visiting places important in the life of Jesus or where there are great centers of Christian learning or prayer. Five of the most popular Christian pilgrimage sites in the world are: the Holy Land (now divided between Israel, Jordan, Palestine, and Syria); Istanbul; the Vatican City in Rome; Santiago de Compostela in Spain; and Lourdes in France. Santiago is believed to be the burial place of St. James, a disciple of Jesus. At Lourdes, a young girl named Bernadette believed she saw Mary, the Mother of God.

Priests at an altar at the pilgrimage site at Lourdes, France. In the background is a statue of Mary, Mother of God.

Protestants

Starting in the 16th century, some Christians protested the practices of the Catholic Church and the Pope's authority. These groups came to be known as "Protestants." The first Protestants were the followers of Martin Luther in Germany, now called Lutherans. There are many Protestant groups today. Among them are the Baptists, Presbyterians, and Methodists. There are also Anglican (Church of England) and Episcopalian churches that form a bridge between the Roman Catholic and Protestant churches. All believe the *Bible* should be studied in a formal (methodical) way, and some believe that only adults should be baptized.

Singing hymns in the First African Baptist Church in the state of Georgia

Quakers

The Religious Society of Friends, or Quakers, were Protestants that were badly treated in England. Some fled to North America—among them were the Pilgrims—where they set up small communities. Today, Quakers are famous for their hard work, nonviolence, and living a simple life. They do not have priests, and silence is a feature of their worship.

The Story of Islam

We are Muslims, followers of Islam. We believe that there is one God, whom we call Allah. "Islam" is an Arabic word that means "to submit." So Muslims are people who submit to Allah's wishes. We believe that Allah sent prophets, including Moses and Jesus, to teach us about Allah's laws. The last and most important of these was the Prophet Muhammad.

The Qur'an (Koran)

We believe that the *Qur'an* (also written as *Koran*) contains the words of Allah, which the angel revealed to Muhammad. Muhammad learned the words by heart, and friends wrote them down for him. The words are in Arabic, and we try to learn them. Muslims treat copies of the *Qur'an* with respect.

Muhammad's vision

Muhammad lived about 1,400 years ago in the city of Makkah (also written as Mecca) in Arabia. He was troubled by the dishonesty and poverty around him. One day he saw an angel holding a cloth with words on it. Muhammad could not read, but the angel helped him to recite the words. The message on the cloth told of the power of Allah, and how Allah should be worshiped.

Muhammad returned to Makkah and began to preach to the people about his wonderful vision.

To read the *Qur'an*, we put it on a stand.

Muhammad's followers pray at the *Ka'ba*, a sacred building in Makkah—just as they do today.

Hajj (Pilgrimage)

The *hajj* is a pilgrimage to Makkah, our holiest city, made at a special time of year. All Muslims should make the journey at least once in their lives. Everyone wears simple clothes. The men wear a white robe, called *ihram*, so they all look equal to one another. Many men cover their heads, and all the women and girls wear veils. When they reach Makkah, the pilgrims worship at several sites, including the *Ka'ba*.

A Muslim family in Egypt have painted their house with scenes from their pilgrimage to Makkah.

Our Duties

We are all expected to give some of our money to charity. It may go to build a hospital, or to help the poor and needy. This giving of alms is called *zakat*, an offering to Allah. It is one of the five main duties in life, which Muslims must practice. These are the Five Pillars of Islam. The other four are *shahada* (declaring faith in Allah), *salat* (praying every day), *sawm* (fasting during Ramadan), and *hajj* (going on a pilgrimage).

We take off our shoes before entering the mosque.

The Call to Prayer

Muslims say prayers five times a day—once in the morning before sunrise, three times during the day, and once at night. At the mosque, our place of worship, a man called the *muezzin* calls us to prayer from a *minaret* (tall tower). At midday every Friday, we go to the mosque to pray.

minaret

muezzin

Being a Muslim

Islam is more than our religion: it is a way of life. For instance, the mosque is our special place to worship Allah, but Muslims can say their daily prayers wherever they are—at work, at home, or at school. Prayer is the most important part of our worship. In our set prayers we bow, kneel, and touch the ground with our foreheads. We always face toward Makkah, and choose some clean ground or use a prayer mat.

In the Mosque

Mosques are often beautifully decorated, but there are no pictures or statues of living things. Muhammad thought that people might worship them instead of Allah. There are no seats, either. The main hall is an open space where the men sit or stand in rows, shoulder to shoulder. Women sit separately, behind the screen on the left. The alcove in the center is called the *mihrab*, and it faces in the exact direction of Makkah. On Fridays, the *imam*, our community leader, gives a sermon from a pulpit called the *minbar*.

Cleansing

To show our respect for Allah, we leave our shoes outside the mosque and enter in bare feet. We also wash ourselves in a special ceremony called *wudu*. There is an area in the mosque set aside for this, with running water. We wash in a set order— the hands and face, then the arms, head, and ears. Lastly, we wash our feet.

Everyday Worship

We have several things that help us in our daily prayer and worship. With a compass, we can find the true direction of Makkah. We kneel on a special mat for our prayers. We study the *Qur'an* throughout our lives, and try to learn its passages by heart. We keep our heads covered when we pray, to show respect to Allah. Women have scarves or veils, and men have caps. And we use a string of beads to help us remember the ninety-nine different names for Allah written in the *Qur'an*.

Skull cap

Qur'an

Stand for *Qur'an*

Prayer mat

Prayer beads

Compass

Ramadan

During the month of Ramadan, Muslims must fast from dawn to dusk. The grown-ups eat breakfast before daylight and then nothing until dinner, after sunset. Part of the reason for Ramadan is to make us aware of the needs of others.

Muslims can eat most kinds of food, but they must not eat pork or drink alcohol. All meat must be prepared in a special way, called *halal*.

Prophets and Angels

Everyday in prayer we say, "There is no god but Allah and Muhammad is his prophet." But Muhammad knew Christian and Jewish teachings, and learned about the prophets. So as prophets, Muslims, too, have Ibrahim (Abraham), Musa (Moses), Dawud (David), and Isa (Jesus). And the angel who told Muhammad to recite is Jibra'il (Gabriel).

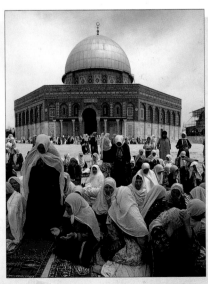

The Dome of the Rock mosque in Jerusalem is sacred to Muslims.

35

The Muslim Year

Each month in the Islamic calendar lasts from one new moon to the next. This means that our months are shorter than ordinary ones. The first month of our year is Muharram. On the ordinary calendar, Muharram starts 10 or 11 days earlier each year.

Maulid al Nabi

This is the Prophet Muhammad's birthday. Many Muslims celebrate all through the third month of our year with processions, speeches, and prayers, and remember the most important events from the Prophet's life. Other Muslims do not make such an elaborate celebration.

Id-ul-Adha

Muslims who are not on *hajj* celebrate the "Feast of Sacrifice." It remembers the moment when Allah asked Ibrahim (Abraham) to sacrifice his son. Some Muslims sacrifice a goat or sheep on the morning of the festival. This story is important to Jews, too (see page 18).

During the last days of Ramadan, some Muslims stay in the mosque for special prayers.

We honor a goat that is to be sacrificed.

Id-ul-Fitr

The end of our period of fasting (Ramadan) is marked by the rising of the new moon, which shows that a new month is starting. We go to the mosque for special prayers, and then the celebrations begin! There are parties and feasts, and we give each other presents.

Children celebrate the Prophet's birthday, dancing in the streets of Mombasa, Kenya.

Ashura

Near the beginning of the Muslim New Year is the festival of Ashura. Muhammad tells us that this was the day when Allah made the world, when Noah's ark landed, and when Jesus was born. Many Muslims fast during Ashura.

For many of our festivals, we make special foods and share them with each other.

Hijrah

After his vision in the desert, Muhammad began telling the people of Makkah about Allah. He said that many of them were living sinful lives. This made Muhammad very unpopular. He decided to move to the nearby city of Medina. There he was made welcome, and founded the first Islamic community. Muhammad's journey is called the *hijrah*, meaning "departure." The success of Muhammad's teaching grew quickly, and his followers soon defeated the people of Makkah. Muhammad returned to the city in triumph.

The Muslim calendar starts from the year that Muhammad moved to Medina (622 C.E.). The year 2000, the Muslim year 1421 starts.

**Dervishes follow poor but strict ways of life.
A part of their worship and remembrances is dancing to pipe music, or whirling—like planets around the sun.**

During Ashura, Muslims celebrate the day when Noah's ark touched ground and Noah and the animals stepped on dry land again.

Growing Up

The Islamic religion is closely linked with every moment of our lives. As soon as Muslims are born, we are made part of the faith. As we grow up, we are taught the ways that Islam can guide us through life. Families are very important, but we are also part of the whole family of believers throughout the world, which is called the *ummah*.

Some Muslims attend Islamic schools.

Birth

The first ceremony takes place as soon as a baby is born. We believe that a child is a gift from Allah, and must be brought into the faith as quickly as possible. The baby is washed, and the call to prayer is whispered in its right ear. A second prayer, the call to worship, is whispered in the baby's left ear. Next, honey or a piece of sugar is placed on the baby's tongue as a sign of a happy life.

Aqiqah (Naming)

This ceremony is held when a baby is seven days old. It is given a Muslim name. Its head is shaved, and silver of the same weight as the shaved hair is given to the poor. Boys are circumcised (see Judaism, page 18).

Reading and Writing

Like all Muslim children, when I was seven years old I went to evening lessons at the mosque. The *imam* taught me how to read the *Qur'an* in Arabic, its original language. I also learned how to write in Arabic letters, and the correct ways to pray and behave in the mosque.

Learning to Be an Adult

By the time we are 13 years old, children are expected to know how to behave in an adult Muslim way. Although we are taught many things in the mosque or at school, home is an important place for learning, too. I help my mother to prepare meals in the correct way, and learn which foods are forbidden. I am taught how to dress modestly and how to keep clean and healthy. All children must show respect for older people, especially their parents. Children are taught to obey their parents—even when they are wrong!

Relatives bring gifts to a new husband and wife in Pakistan.

Marriage

A Muslim wedding is usually a lot of fun, with a party and colorful clothes. Many marriages are arranged by the bride's father, although our law says that a woman cannot be forced to marry someone she does not want to. The wedding ceremony is not a religious one. The man proposes marriage and his bride accepts before witnesses. They both sign a contract to make it legal, and the man gives his bride a sum of money.

Death and Burial

When a person dies, the body is wrapped in white sheets and buried as soon as possible. Friends call on the family to show their respect and support. Muslims believe that one day the dead will be raised to life and judged by Allah. Those who have lived good lives will go to Paradise. Others will go into everlasting fire.

Islam Around the World

Islam began as a religion of the Middle East, in Saudi Arabia. Today, worldwide, there are more than one billion Muslims. Most Muslims live in the Middle East, North Africa, southeastern Europe, and Southeast Asia. In Europe and the Americas, the number of Muslims is still small but is growing fast.

At prayer in the street in Cairo, Egypt

The Sunnis

Four out of every five Muslims are from the Sunni branch of Islam. The Sunnis believe that Muslim leaders should be elected by the people. Sunni Muslims follow the traditional practices of the Prophet Muhammad. The word Sunni means "majority" and Sunnis set the standards for Muslim life and practice. These include the rules for forbidden foods, fasting, and personal hygiene.

The Shi'as

Shi'a Muslims believe that the leaders of their communities must be related through history to Muhammad's cousins and son-in-law, Ali. Such leaders are powerful and are often seen as energetic seekers after truth. They have a strong tradition of dying for their faith. Iran is the best known Shi'ite nation, where religious and political rule are one and the same.

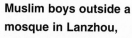

Muslim boys outside a mosque in Lanzhou, China

Sufis

A small branch of Islam is Sufism. These Muslims use music, drumming, and dance in their worship. The Dervishes (see page 37) belong to this group. Most Sufis live in Turkey.

These Arab Bedouin are celebrating the end of Ramadan.

Islam in Europe and America

The strong belief of Islam—that the word of Allah is delivered in the *Qur'an*—often makes it difficult for Muslims to live in Western society. Islam is a way of life, with daily customs, traditions, and rituals that do not easily fit in countries where most people belong to and practice other religions.

The Nation of Islam

In the United States in the 1930s, a Black religious leader, Elijah Muhammad, started a movement called the Black Muslims, or the Nation of Islam. These Muslims had their own beliefs. One of their followers was Malcolm X. He persuaded many of them to accept Muslim beliefs as taught elsewhere in the world. The Nation of Islam continues, led by Minister Louis Farrakhan, who has a small following.

These Muslim women in Pakistan are wearing *yashmaks*—veils that completely cover the face.

Muslim Dress

People who have changed their religion to Islam often wear Asian or Arabic clothes as a symbol of their new faith. However, many Muslims who live in or come from Asia and the Middle East wear Western dress, such as jeans and shirts. In fact, the *Qur'an* only says that Muslims should not dress to show off or impress one another. For many Muslims, men covering the head and women wearing a veil are ways of being modest and equal to everyone else.

Being a Hindu

Our religion is a major religion of India. It has no founder. Hinduism includes many ancient religious beliefs and customs. There is no single book. Our sacred books contain stories, hymns, prayers, and poems. As Hindus we must say our prayers, worship our gods and goddesses, and try to live as good a life as we can. If we do it well, we believe we will be reborn into a better life. This is called reincarnation.

Signs and Symbols

The most famous Hindu symbol is *Aum*, or "Om." It means "everything"—past, present, and future. Other symbols include animals associated with gods and goddesses, such as the bull Nandi with Shiva. In India, cows are sacred and are treated with great respect. Hindus are mainly vegetarian and do not eat beef.

Hindu Gods

We worship many gods and goddesses. They are all different forms of one supreme God. One god, Krishna, is much loved because of his tricks and teasing. As a young man, he once took the clothes of some beautiful girls. He put them up in a tree, and made the girls come and get them back. Hindus say the story means we must come to God as if we were naked and not hide things from him. Krishna is often seen playing the flute.

Rama   Krishna

Hanuman   Durga

Ganesh   Lakshmi

I am holding a statue of the god Shiva.

The photo at left shows holy men chanting hymns. The marks on their foreheads represent the god Vishnu.

Shrines

Everywhere in India, in cities, in villages, and by the roadsides, there are shrines. There are many temples, too, but the main religious life of Hindus is in the home. In Hindu communities in other countries, the *mandir*, or temple, is often a place for meetings as well as a house of worship.

Pilgrimage

Many places in India are famous because they are connected with the lives of the Hindu gods. Most of us will make a pilgrimage to a holy place some time in our lives. One of the best known holy places is Benares. Here we bathe in the holy waters of the Ganges River and say our prayers. This is our religious duty and we hope it will deepen our faith. At pilgrimage sites, we often meet *gurus*. These holy men are Hindu priests or teachers. They carry out religious duties, chanting the prayers and scriptures.

Worship at Home

We have a shrine in our house for daily worship, which we call *puja*. We sing a prayer and say the holy names of God. Our shrine has a statue of Krishna and a small statue of Ganesh for good luck. In front of our shrine we place incense, a bowl of water, a bell and a flower. Other Hindus also put an *Aum* symbol, a *mandala* for meditation, prayer beads and food to be shared. All these items are to show that everything is offered to God.

Incense sticks

***Aum* symbol**

Statue of goddess

Bell

Offerings of fruit, petals and sweets

43

Customs and Festivals

Hindus are born into four main groups—*brahmin*, *kshatriya*, *vaishya*, and *shudras*. Each has its own customs and traditions, but we all have similar ceremonies to mark the important events in our lives.

Marriage

Parents often choose the person their son or daughter will marry because the marriage is between two families, not just the couple. At the marriage service the couple sit under a canopy. Their right hands are joined by a yellow thread. They walk three times around a small fire. They then take seven steps together—to represent food, strength, wealth, good luck, children, the seasons, and lasting friendship.

Starting a New Life

A birth is a new start. The baby is washed, his or her head is shaved, and the *Aum* symbol is traced on the tongue with honey. At about 12 years old, Brahmin boys take part in a "sacred thread" ceremony. Cotton threads are looped over the boy's head and tied with a knot. The boy is given a sacred staff. He gives his *guru*, or teacher, a garland of flowers.

Brahmin boy with sacred thread.

Death

In Hinduism the body is burned, usually within 24 hours of death. The dead body is washed and wrapped in a cloth. A close relative—a son, if there is one—lights the fire. After the ceremony the ashes are collected and sprinkled in a river. Hindus believe that when the body has been burned the soul can be reincarnated in another body.

Holi (Late February)

Holi is a spring festival popular in north India. It lasts for two or three days. It celebrates the tricks of Krishna's boyhood. There are noisy processions and people spray one another with water and colored powder. A bonfire is lit and coconuts are roasted. Some Hindus celebrate Holi by carrying their babies and young children around the bonfire.

Dassehra (September)

This is the north Indian name for a festival at the end of the monsoon, the season of heavy rains. On each of nine nights, a different form of the goddess Durga is celebrated. On the last day, a figure of the demon king Ravana is set on fire to show Durga's triumph over demons.

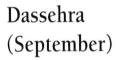

Janamashtami (Early September)

This is the birthday of Krishna. He is said to have been born at midnight. Many Hindus stay up late at night as if to welcome the baby. In some homes, a statue of Krishna is placed on a swing or cradle during the festival.

Divali (October/November)

This is the weeklong festival of lights when we light oil lamps to invite the blessing of Lakshmi, the goddess of wealth. It is the time when shopkeepers work out their annual accounts and pay their debts. They pray for a good year and good business next year. People decorate their homes with flowers and offer sweet foods.

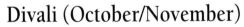

Being a Buddhist

We believe that our founder, Buddha, shows us the way to live. Buddha was a man named Siddhartha Gautama. He did not believe in a god, and we do not worship the Buddha. We pay respect to him and try to follow his teachings. Buddhists are concerned for all living things. We do not eat meat and we believe in treating humans and animals with respect.

A Buddhist monk makes an offering under a sacred tree in Sri Lanka.

Nirvana

Nirvana is the aim of Buddhists. It is a feeling of joy and freedom. We believe it is also the end of the cycle of birth, death, and rebirth. Buddhists believe death is not the end of life: it is only another step on the way. Everyone will have many lives and many deaths.

Death
Illness
Old age
Birth
Nirvana

The Eightfold Path

An eight-spoked wheel is the symbol of Buddhism. It remembers the eight steps Buddha spoke about at his first sermon to show people the way to live. His speech is called the Sermon of the Turning of the Wheel.

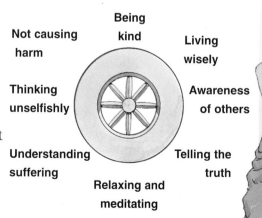

Being kind
Not causing harm
Living wisely
Thinking unselfishly
Awareness of others
Understanding suffering
Telling the truth
Relaxing and meditating

Buddha's Life

Siddhartha Gautama lived about 2,500 years ago in north India. He was a prince, protected from the problems of everyday life. Then he set out to look for a way to end the suffering that comes to everyone. He meditated, and thought deeply about his life. He reached an understanding, or "enlightenment," and shared this by teaching others his beliefs.

Siddhartha saw four signs that sent him on his search: a sick man, an old man, a dead man, and a holy man.

Meditation

This is needed to reach *nirvana*. It involves deep religious thought and concentration, which is hard and needs years of practice. To help them meditate, some Buddhists stare for hours at an object like a disk, or say a word over and over again. Others stare at a *thanka*, an embroidered cloth with symbols on it. Monasteries and temples have a room where people can come and meditate. Sometimes people stay at special meditation centers.

Prayer

Many Buddhists do not pray, because there is no god to pray to. In Tibet there are "prayer wheels" and "prayer flags" to spin or wave, as if to spread good thoughts out into the world.

A hand-held prayer wheel

Items used at shrines in homes to help meditation include:
– a picture or statue of Buddha
– small bells
– bowls of water
– sticks of incense, which give off a pleasant smell when burned
– a *tharka*.

Becoming a Monk

In countries such as Nepal and Tibet, a Buddhist boy will become a monk for a few months to help him reach enlightenment. His parents take him to the joining ceremony. His head is shaved and he is given a monk's robe. This is usually orange or red in color. His parents gain merit by doing this and by treating him with respect. Buddhist girls may become nuns for a short time in a similar way.

Giant prayer wheels at a nunnery in Nepal

47

Customs and Festivals

The *sangha*, or monastery, is important to us, and we go there to celebrate festivals. In each *sangha* is a shrine with a beautiful statue of Buddha. We put offerings, such as flowers, lighted candles, and incense, in front of the shrine. Often, parents will take their newborn baby to the *sangha* to be blessed by a monk. When Buddhists marry, they go to the *sangha* to be blessed.

Giving and being generous to other people is part of being a Buddhist.

Statues of Buddha inside a *pagoda*

The Dalai Lama

The Dalai Lama is one of Buddhism's great teachers today. He was the Buddhist leader in Tibet until the Chinese stopped all religion there. He now lives in India, but travels widely all over the world.

Sacred Places

Our temples are places where great Buddhist masters are buried or where relics of the Buddha are kept. Often the temples are bell-shaped *stupas* or tall *pagodas*. To help Buddhists meditate, images of Buddha are kept in the temple. The images usually show him sitting cross-legged. The Buddha's hands may be held in different ways, to mean meditation, giving, or achieving enlightenment. Some mountains and trees in Nepal and Tibet are also sacred places for Buddhists.

The Dalai Lama speaking to Buddhists

48

The Year

Most Buddhist festivals are celebrated at the time of a full moon or new moon. In different places, events like Buddha's birth are celebrated at different times and in different ways. Everywhere, the festivals are times to be kind to people, to feed the poor, and to gain much merit.

At Songkran—New Year in Thailand— we follow Buddha's teaching about being kind to living things.

Buddhist women dance to celebrate the New Year in China.

New Year (March/April)

This is a time for cleaning and washing away bad deeds. In Thailand, Buddhists give monks and nuns lots of food. In Sri Lanka, people bring flowers to the Temple of the Buddha's Tooth. In Japan, at midnight, bells are rung. Each ring is supposed to drive out one of our faults. Buddhists try to think how they can lead better lives.

Wesak or Vesakha (May/June)

This celebrates the birth, enlightenment, and death of the Buddha—all three in one day! People send each other greeting cards and decorate the local temple with lights. Some Buddhists meditate all through the night.

Asalha Perahara (July/August)

This is a famous festival in Kandy in Sri Lanka. Monks do not take part, but they do watch the procession of 100 elephants and dancers and drummers in wonderful costumes. The Buddha's tooth is taken through the streets of the city in a special casket.

Being a Sikh

Sikhism was founded in north India about 500 years ago by a young man, Guru Nanak. To be a Sikh is to follow the teachings of the ten *gurus* (great Sikh teachers). We believe in one God, and that humans are all equal. When we are 15 years old, we can join the *khalsa*, the community of Sikhs. We also take *amrit*, a ceremony in which we promise to follow the Sikh teaching.

Guru Nanak

He was brought up as a Hindu. He was a special person, and made friends with the ruling Muslims. He was known as a great spiritual teacher. His followers lived and ate together to show everyone was equal. A saying of Guru Nanak is, "Truth is high, but higher still is truthful living."

The Five Ks

Sikh men wear a *turban*, a cloth wrapped around the head. It is like a badge; everyone can see it. They also wear the five symbols of our faith to show they belong to the *khalsa* (community). These are the five Ks— each symbol begins with the letter K. They are:

Kesh—uncut hair (hair and beard are left to grow).
Kangha—a small comb, to keep the hair in place.
Kirpan—a dagger, to remind Sikhs to fight for what is right and protect others.
Kara—a bangle, to remind Sikhs of the oneness of God.
Kacchera—shorts or pants, usually worn as underwear.

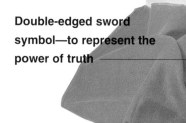

Double-edged sword symbol—to represent the power of truth

kirpan on belt

kacchera

In the Gurdwara

Gurdwara means "door of the Guru" and is the Sikh place of worship. Most important, it is the home of the *Guru Granth Sahib*, our holy book. Sikhs gather together in *gurdwara* around the holy book. Worship consists of singing songs from the holy book, reading from it, and listening to a sermon based on one of its stories. On entering the *gurdwara*, we remove our shoes and cover our heads to show respect. We go up to the holy book, bow down, and make an offering—perhaps money or food or milk. Then we sit on the floor, women and girls on one side, men and boys on the other. People come and go, as the worship can last many hours.

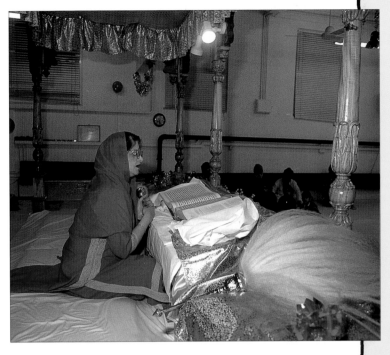

A Sikh woman reads from the *Guru Granth Sahib*.

The Guru Granth Sahib

The holy book is placed under a special canopy. The *granthi* (reader) waves a *chouri* (fan) over it, to show how important the book is. Anyone may come to read from the book, but it is regarded as an honor. The holy book contains the teachings of the *gurus*.

The *Guru Granth Sahib* is placed on a bookrest.

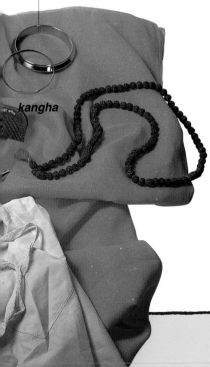

Steel *kara*

kangha

The Langar

The *gurdwara* is also a social center. There is a *langar* (kitchen), where meals are often prepared by members of the *khalsa*. The meals are shared by everyone. It is an act of love and caring for all people. In the *langar*, the community eat together, talk, play music, and enjoy each other's friendship. This sense of belonging to one family is a strong part of the Sikh religion.

Customs and Festivals

Sikhs consider their faith part of normal life. We believe in giving service to the community by working in the *gurdwara*, or running clubs for the whole community. There is no special day in the week for worship. Many Sikhs say daily prayers, usually by reading passages from the *Guru Granth Sahib* that most of us keep at home.

Naming a Baby

We take my baby sister to the *gurdwara* to give thanks to God and to say prayers for her well-being. We listen eagerly for the first word read from the *Guru Granth Sahib*. Its first letter will decide the letter that begins her name. It's a P, so we call her Pritam. She will also be called *Kaur*, meaning princess. A baby boy would be called *Singh* (lion). Using these common names means we all belong to one family of Sikhs.

Amritsar

The Golden Temple at Amritsar was built by Arjan. He was the fifth *guru* and lived about 100 years after Nanak. Most Sikhs try to visit this temple at some time in their lives. It is beautiful and surrounded by water. Bathing in the water is of special religious importance. The temple is open on all four sides. This is to show it is open to everyone to visit and pray.

Marriage

Sikh families help young people to choose their partner. The marriage ceremony follows a set pattern. The bride's father brings garlands for the bride, the groom, and the *Guru Granth Sahib*. He ties his daughter's head scarf to the shawl that the groom wears. Then the bride and groom walk four times round the holy book.

Death

Sikhs believe in rebirth, or reincarnation. When a Sikh dies, his or her body is cremated.

A Sikh man is taken to the funeral ground wearing the five Ks. The ashes of the body are thrown into flowing water, either a stream or a river. All the mourners wear white clothes. After the funeral, in the *gurdwara*, the whole *Guru Granth Sahib* may be read. This takes several days. During this time, the mourners go to the *gurdwara* as often as they can. Each day a meal is served in the *langar*.

Hola Mohalla (February/March)

This is at the same time as the Hindu festival of Holi (page 45). Sikhs hold contests and show their skills at athletics, horsemanship, and martial arts. The largest gathering of Sikhs is where the *khalsa* was founded, at Anandpur in India.

Divali (October)

At this four-day festival the story of Hargobind (the sixth *guru*) is told. He refused to leave prison until fifty-two Indian Hindu princes were also set free. It is a festival we share with Hindus. We light candles and the *gurdwaras* are lit up with electric lights or oil lamps. Children are given presents by their relatives. We light fireworks, and there is much noise and happiness.

Baisakhi (March/April)

In the Punjab, in north India, this is New Year's Day. It celebrates the day when Guru Gobind Singh (the tenth *guru*) founded the *khalsa*. It is held on April 13. The *Amrit* ceremony for joining the *khalsa* often takes place on Baisakhi. In the city of Amritsar there is a great animal fair at this time.

Guru Nanak's Birthday (October/November)

This is an important day in the Sikh year. It is held shortly after Divali. The *Guru Granth Sahib* is carried through the streets by five men, to represent the first five Sikhs who were prepared to die for Guru Nanak. There are music and speeches, and much happiness. When we return to the *gurdwara*, the *Guru Granth Sahib* is read.

53

Being Shinto

My religion means "the way of the gods." It is practiced only in Japan. It is much older than Buddhism. We believe the Japanese islands were specially created by the gods. We have a strong belief in the power of *kami* (spirits), and respect for our elders and leaders. Many Japanese people think of themselves as both Buddhist and Shinto.

Worship

There are lots of gods in Shinto. To worship them, people have built shrines high in the mountains. Every village has its shrine or temple. Some shrines are huge—we call them god-houses. In the very center of the shrine is the "god-body." This is something very simple like a mirror or a pebble. It shows our belief that spiritual powers exist in everything in nature—rocks, the wind, plants, animals, and people, including the dead. Only our priests can go into this very special area. Our home has a *kami-dana*, a little shrine where we worship every day. We offer rice, salt, water, and, on special days, fruit and other food to honor the *kami*.

Our Traditions

The major beliefs of Shinto are the importance of family traditions and being part of the local community. In our family, when a baby is born or a person marries or dies we hold Shinto ceremonies with our relatives, friends, and neighbors. We go to our local shrine to pray and worship.

Before we enter the shrine, we rinse our mouths and wash our hands. This is to purify ourselves.

This is how the priests call up our *kami*—by striking a big drum.

54

Festivals and Celebrations

Festivals in Japan mean a lot of rituals and bring good cheer. *Matsuri* means both daily worship and special festival times. New Year's Day is one of the biggest *matsuri*. *Kami* are called up through dancing, music, and chanting. Each shrine has a special day for its *kami*. The *kami* is carried about the area bringing new life.

Cherry Blossom Festival (April)

Cherry blossom time has long been celebrated in Japan. The blossom is for us a symbol of pride and hope. Many of the best blossom trees are at old Shinto shrines or holy mountains, such as Mount Fuji. We go into the parks, drink rice wine, and have a good time.

Chichibu Night Festival (December)

This is a famous festival. Huge floats, including a decorated box believed to contain a *kami*, are pulled through the streets. It is great watching the floats being pulled up the last steep slope to the shrine. Behind the floats come the Shinto priests. Fireworks burst over our heads. The strange and wonderful things happen all around us.

Carrying a box with a *kami* to a lake to bring new life to the area

Shichi-go-san

This means seven-five-three. It is celebrated when girls are 7 or 3 years old and boys are 5 years old. We dress up in new clothes and we are taken to the shrine. We and our parents pray that we will grow up healthy and strong. It is a traditional festival but not everyone joins in, and there is no special holiday.

A Shinto girl at her Shichi-go-san ceremony. She is wearing a *kimono*, a Japanese robe that is tied at the back with a sash.

55

☯ Being Taoist

Tao (pronounced "Dow") is the Chinese character for "path" or "way." We can choose to follow a path in life that shows us that one natural force links all things. We have many sacred books. Our best-known is the *Tao-Te-Ching*, which we believe was written over 1,000 years ago. Taoists try to lead good lives and not do evil to anyone. We look after the sick and feed the hungry. We care about nature and the beauty of the world.

Yin and Yang

This harmony is expressed in the *yin-yang* symbol. *Yin* is female, *yang* is male—opposites that come together as one. We believe that *yin* is born on the longest day of summer, *yang* on the shortest day of winter. The seasons of the year are part of one cycle, like the life-cycle of living beings, or the festivals we celebrate each year.

A Taoist monastery in China. The *yin* and *yang* symbol is painted on the right-hand wall. Priests stand in the courtyard.

Sacred Places and Worship

There are five mountains in China sacred to Taoists. Tao monks and nuns live in monasteries close by the mountains. Tao priests often live in temples in the cities. All these teachers of our religion meditate to try to reach harmony through a simple life. Some eat only vegetables. Many do not cut their hair, but tie it in a knot. Most priests are married. Some live at home, then go to the monastery for a while, then return home again.

Tai-Chi

This looks like exercises but it is much more than that. *Tai* means strength or power that is in everything. *Chi* is the flow of energy. When we practice *tai-chi*, we bring together this inner strength and energy, making them one force. We concentrate on movement and breathing, as in meditation.

Confucianism

Confucius was a writer who lived 2,500 years ago. He wrote advice for China's rulers. He taught that *Tao*—the belief in oneness or harmony—comes from order and respect for others, and that goodness and love follow from correct behavior.

Festivals and Celebrations

The Chinese love festivals! We have wonderful processions, especially at their New Year, which falls in February. It is also the time the kitchen god visits to report on the family, so statues of him and other charms are put up. Good-luck sayings are hung over doorways. At the midautumn festival, thousands of lanterns are lit.

Dragon Boat Festival (June)

This honors an official, Ch'u Yuan, who was so fed up with the emperor's unkindness that he drowned himself. Dragon boat races are held to recall the dash to save his body. It is said that a dumpling was thrown into the sea so the fish would not eat him. Dumplings are still made and eaten during the festival.

Hungry Ghosts Festival (August/September)

Demons and ghosts are important in Taoism. In stories, priests often fight them. At this time of year, we imagine that gates to the underworld are open and ghosts wander out. Some ghosts are unhappy because they may have no family to honor or look after them. The festival is held to give these unhappy ghosts offerings of money, paper houses, fruit, and clothes. In some places, small fires are lit so the offerings can be brought and burned on the fire.

57

Some Other Faiths

Being a Jain

I am a member of a small Indian religion. We believe that everything we do has a good or bad effect on our lives, and that we are reborn. We believe in *ahimsa* (nonviolence), so we do not kill animals. We are strict vegetarians.

Some of our monks wear a face mask, strain drinking water, and brush the road in front of them as they walk. This is so they will not kill any living thing, however small, even by accident. You can become a monk as young as eight years old.

Nearly every Jain town has a temple and most of us have a shrine in our homes. We decorate these with flowers and with statues of our great Jain teachers. Our big festivals are Jayanti, the birth of Mahavira, the founder of Jainism, and Paryushana-pana, the ending of the rainy season.

Jains celebrate Jayanti, carrying a statue of Mahavira through the streets

Being a Baha'i

We believe in the oneness of the human race. There is a Baha'i saying, "You are the fruits of the same tree." For us, God is revealed to different peoples in different ways, according to when we live. He does this through prophets and writings. He might be Moses, Jesus, Buddha, Mohammad, or Vishnu—and each is right for his time. For our present time, Baha'is believe the writings of Abdul Baha and Baha'u'llah (both born in Iran in the 19th century) are sacred. Baha'is live in many countries, but our main center is in Haifa, Israel.

Being a Rastafarian

My religion takes its name from *Ras Tafari*. It means Lion of Judah. This was the title given to Haile Selassie, the last emperor of Ethiopia in North Africa. Ethiopia, a Christian country, had fought against rule by Europeans. People who came originally from Africa, such as many West Indians, think of Ethiopia as a homeland and that Haile Selassie was a *messiah*, or messenger, sent by God to teach us how to live. There is a tradition in the Book of Leviticus, in the *Bible*, that hair should not be cut. We wear our hair long, in dreadlocks.

Rastafarian father and daughter

Being a Zoroastrian

I am a Parsi and follow the teaching of Zoroaster (Zarathustra). It is said he was the only baby who laughed instead of cried at birth. Parsi means people from Persia (now called Iran), and our ancestors migrated from there to India more than 1,000 years ago. We believe we are each responsible for our actions, both good and bad. People whose deeds are good go to Paradise, but people who do bad things go to the House of the Lie when they die.

Zoroastrians hold many rituals in search of purity. Fire is a symbol of their God.

New Religions

Some religions, like those of ancient Egypt, can disappear. New religions, such as Cao Dai, can be born. The last 100 years has seen the development of several new cults, or religious ideas. These cults are often called New Age religions. Some express concern for nature. Others are reactions against an excessive desire for money and possessions. A few cults are based on "lost" religions, such as those of the American Indians.

Followers of Cao Dai in a temple in Vietnam. Cao Dai was founded in 1926.

One Big Family

As we have described and shown in this book, there are many different religions in the world. Some religions are practiced in many countries by millions of people. Others are limited to only a few countries and have far fewer followers. Each religion has its own customs and traditions. As long as we respect each other's beliefs and allow people to practice their religion freely, the world should be a happier place. Religion can help us to live together like brothers and sisters.

Some people dream of a time when all the religions of the world will agree with one another, work together, and be one. All religions value human life. They also believe that certain times, places, and events are sacred or special. But they disagree about whether or not there is a god and which god to follow. However, most religions also teach us to love others and to make friends. So as you grow up, let your religion help you learn about each other and work and play together.

Glossary

alms gifts of money or food to poor people.

ancestor a relative in the distant past from whom someone is descended.

calendar a system for dividing up time. In the Jewish and Muslim calendars, months last from one new moon to the next. These months are shorter than ordinary months by a day or two.

ceremony traditional religious ritual or occasion.

chanting singing or saying the same words or phrases over and over again.

community people sharing a common religion.

cremation burning the body after death. Hindus, Sikhs, and some Christians do this.

cult religious ideas fashionable within a small group.

custom practice that has become regular or standard. Custom plays a major part in all religions.

divine related to God or other gods and goddesses.

enlightenment in Buddhism, reaching a deep understanding and peace of mind.

evil badness, harm, or wrongdoing.

faith trust in God or in the power of religion.

festival a celebration to mark a religious event.

guru Hindu or Sikh religious teacher.

hymn a religious song of praise.

laws rules for followers of a religion. Different religions have different laws.

meditation deep concentration to free the mind of unwanted thoughts.

merit entitlement to a reward in the future. Buddhists believe that, after death, this may lead to being reborn into a better life.

monastery a place away from the outside world where religious men, called monks, go to live and study their religion in peace and quiet. Women who live like this are called nuns and their home is the nunnery.

mystical mysterious, difficult for humans to understand.

nonviolence not using force. Believers in nonviolence refuse to kill, to injure, or to fight in wars. Jains are such strict believers that they even avoid treading on insects.

orthodox applying religious teachings (doctrine) rigidly in all circumstances. There are Orthodox Christians and Orthodox Jews.

pagoda Buddhist temple built as a tower in several tiers, with an upward-turned roof at each tier.

paradise a place where everything is perfect; heaven.

persecution attacking people, killing them, or driving them from their homes because of their religion or race.

pilgrimage journey to a holy or sacred place. People who go on pilgrimages are called pilgrims.

prayer request or thanks to God or other gods or spirits.

preach tell people about God and the power of religion.

priest person appointed to carry out religious duties, such as teaching and leading services in the house of worship and prayer.

prophet very wise or holy man who passes on messages from God.

rabbi Jewish teacher of the Jewish religion and law.

reincarnation rebirth in a new body. Buddhists, Hindus, and Sikhs believe in reincarnation.

relics remains such as the bones of a prophet or saint, or bits of their belongings.

respect high regard for someone or something. It might be a person, or persons, living or dead, a custom or tradition, or even the whole of nature. Most religions are built on respect in some form or other.

resurrection being raised from the dead. Christians believe in the resurrection of Christ.

ritual a repeated pattern of actions, as religious rituals performed during a service or ceremony.

sacred holy, precious, or important to followers of a religion. For example, the Koran is sacred to Muslims.

sacrifice killing of an animal as an offering to a god or goddess.

saint in the Catholic Church, a person officially recognized as special because of their religious deeds or holy experiences; to Protestants, any true believer in Christ or anyone who does good religious works or deeds.

scripture sacred writing.

sermon religious speech with a message about right and wrong or how people should live their lives.

service meeting of Jews, Christians, or others to praise their God or gods.

shrine sacred building or other sacred place, or a container of sacred objects.

soul the part of the person, some religions believe, that does not die when the body dies.

stained glass glass that has been stained or colored. Stained-glass windows are found in many Christian churches and often show scenes from the Bible.

standing stones large stones put up by people in ancient times. They might have had some religious meaning, but this is not certain.

stupa Buddhist temple shaped like a bell.

suffering experiencing pain or distress. Christians believe that Jesus suffered and died to save the world. Buddhists believe that suffering is caused by desire and can be overcome.

symbol anything—a special food, a piece of jewelry, an article of clothing—that has a religious or traditional meaning.

temple building where worship takes place.

totem pole a pole, carved or painted with animals, representing the family line. Totem poles were used by the American Indians, who believed they kept evil spirits away.

tradition way of thinking or behaving that is handed down from generation to generation.

vegetarian someone who does not eat meat. Buddhists and Jains are strict vegetarians.

worship adoring a god, gods, or spirits.

Index